Rich...
King of C...

The skull of King Richard III
(University of Leicester)
Front cover: 15th Century Portrait of Richard III by an unknown artist.
(National Portrait Gallery)

RICHARD III KING OF CONTROVERSY

Richard III
King of Controversy

ISBN: 978-0955592522
First Published in 2013 by
Echoes from History

Richard III King of Controversy

TONI MOUNT

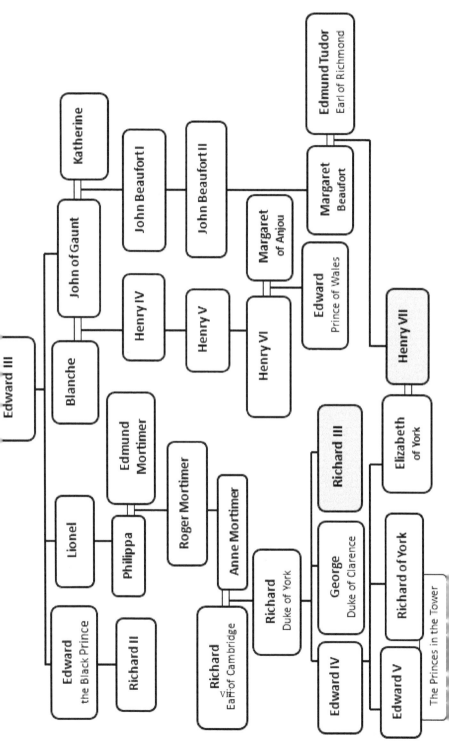

Contents

Richard Duke of Gloucester

Richard was born at Fotheringhay Castle in North-amptonshire on 2nd October 1452. His father was Richard, Duke of York, and his mother was Cecily Neville, known as the Rose of Raby because she was so beautiful. Richard was the eleventh of their twelve children, though not all the children survived to grow up.

1452 saw the start of the Wars of the Roses – the House of York (Richard's family and friends) against the House of Lancaster (Henry VI who was king at the time and his supporters). Henry was a hopeless king who had mental problems and went mad for months at a time. The Duke of York was his nearest adult male cousin and whenever the king suffered a breakdown, the duke would have to step in.

The king's French wife, Queen Margaret of Anjou, and his cronies didn't like it when York took charge because they couldn't boss him around like they did the king and couldn't have their own way. Every time the king recovered, York was banished to Ireland, out of the country. The result was what they called the 'Cousins' War'.

So young Richard grew up in troubled times. Just after Christmas 1460, his father and Richard's teen-aged brother Edmund were killed at the battle of Wakefield and Richard, aged eight, and his eleven-year-old brother George were smuggled to safety on a ship bound for Burgundy (part of modern Belgium). By March, his eldest brother Edward, the new Duke of York, had defeated the Lancastrians at the battles of Mortimer's Cross and Towton – fought on Palm Sunday 1461 in a snowstorm – and been proclaimed king as Edward IV of the House of York. Richard and George came home. They were made royal dukes and Knights of the Garter at Windsor.

After dotty old Henry, Edward looked perfect as king – nineteen, very tall, handsome, the victor in battle and unmarried; he was the most eligible bachelor in Europe. Little Richard adored his eldest brother but George was jealous: if only he had been born first, he would now be king but, for the present at least, he was his brother's heir. Edward loved the ladies and in Europe discussions were going on to find him a suitable bride. But Edward had his own ideas and on 1st May 1464, he secretly married a pretty widow, Elizabeth Woodville-Grey. He kept her a secret until September when she told him she was pregnant, then everyone had to be informed, in case the baby was a boy and the king's next heir. The child was a girl but by then the secret was out.

The marriage upset a lot of very important people, especially brother George, Duke of Clarence, who knew he wasn't likely to be the king's heir for much longer – a boy was bound to be born next time. Another enraged nobleman was the king's cousin, Richard Neville, Earl of Warwick. He had been in France, negotiating with the King of France for a bride for Edward on the very day Edward had secretly married Elizabeth. He felt insulted. Things got worse when Warwick thought about finding wealthy, noble husbands for his two daughters, Isabel and Anne. The new queen had too many sisters, all needing suitably rich husbands, and King Edward had married the girls off to all the eligible noble young men of England, until only two suitable husbands were left: the king's brothers, George, Duke of Clarence, and Richard, Duke of Gloucester.

In 1468/9, Warwick told the king that Isabel would marry George and Anne would marry Richard – perfect – except the king refused to allow it because he thought Warwick was too proud, arrogant and self-important already and becoming father-in-law to both Edward's male heirs (he still didn't have a son at this time) was just too much. Warwick defied the king and George married Isabel but Richard turned down the offer of marrying Anne because the king had refused permission.

Warwick's defiance of the king became all-out rebellion, with George siding with his new father-in-law who promised him, when Edward was removed from the throne, England would have King George I. Briefly, it seemed they would succeed when Edward became Warwick's prisoner but young Richard and Edward's best friend and chamberlain William, Lord Hastings, rallied support for the imprisoned king and Warwick had to let him go. But now, guilty of treason against the king, Warwick had nothing left to lose and decided to try again, this time with more powerful allies: the French.

The French king agreed to support Warwick in deposing King Edward but not so that George could be king. Instead, the King of France demanded that Warwick should put old mad King Henry back on the throne and make an alliance with the king's French wife, Queen Margaret of Anjou. She was in exile in France with her son, Edward of Lancaster, and to seal the alliance the prince would marry Warwick's younger daughter Anne. Warwick agreed: if Isobel wasn't married to a future king, then Anne would be and he didn't mind which of his daughters would one day be queen. But of course George thought otherwise.

Warwick invaded England with French support and King Edward had to flee for his life. He sailed to

Burgundy, where his sister Margaret was married to the duke. His brother Richard, Lord Hastings and a handful of other loyal men went with the king, sailing on 2nd October 1470 – Richard's eighteenth birthday. The story goes that they had to pay the ship's captain with their jewellery and a fur cloak. Charles, Duke of Burgundy, wasn't interested in his wife's penniless brothers seeking safety in his lands until he discovered that, as part of Warwick's deal with the King of France, England was now preparing to assist the French in an invasion of Burgundy. Edward had always been Burgundy's ally, so it was suddenly important to Charles to get Edward back on the English throne and he was willing to supply an army to do it. The early spring of 1471 saw young Richard rushing frantically around the ports of Holland, persuading ships' captains to transport men, horses and weapons across the North Sea to England. Edward landed in the north of England, in what is now Humberside.

He marched south, Englishmen hurrying to join his army so it grew larger every day. Warwick was in Coventry but failed to come out and challenge Edward as he marched by on his way to London. And there was more good news: while Edward had been in Burgundy, his queen had given birth to a son and heir at last, and Richard persuaded their brother George to change sides and support Edward; after all, George had little chance of being king now, whichever side he was on. The three brothers faced Warwick at the battle of Barnet, just north of London, on 14th April 1471 with Richard being given command of the vanguard. The fighting took place in thick fog and Richard was slightly wounded but two of his squires, Thomas and Miles, died at his side. Warwick was defeated and killed but, on the same day, Queen Margaret of Anjou, her son Edward of Lancaster and his new wife, Anne, Warwick's daughter, landed with a second army in the West Country.

Just three weeks later, King Edward, with Richard again at his side, defeated Margaret's army at the battle of Tewkesbury on 4th May. Edward of Lancaster was killed and his wife, Anne, was widowed. She and Margaret became Edward's prisoners. George was there at Tewkesbury but the king didn't trust him enough to give him a command.

Before he rebelled, the Earl of Warwick had been powerful in the north of England and Edward now needed a reliable, able administrator and commander to take charge there. Richard was the perfect choice but he would have to win the loyalty of the northern lords who had always supported Warwick. The king had the answer: Richard would marry Warwick's now-widowed daughter Anne. She was still only a teenager and was living with George and Isabel, her elder sister. The two girls were now wealthy heiresses since their father's death at Barnet and, in medieval times, that meant their husbands would get all the property and riches. George had no intension of sharing Warwick's wealth with Richard, if he married Anne.

First he tried telling everyone Anne was pregnant with Edward of Lancaster's baby, so Richard couldn't marry her. Then he tried persuading her to go into a convent. Finally, she disappeared from his London home. George denied knowing where she had gone, saying she had run away. We shall probably never know the whole truth but the story is that Richard searched London for Anne and finally found her, washing dishes in a cookshop. He rescued her and took her to sanctuary in the abbey of St Martin le Grand in London, where George couldn't get to her.

King Edward arranged for Richard and Anne to be married but, because they were cousins – Richard's mother and Warwick's father had been sister and brother – they needed special permission (called a 'dispensation') from the Pope. Even now, George tried to stop the wedding by bribing the Pope not to grant the dispensation, but the couple were quietly married anyway, in St Stephen's Chapel, Westminster, trusting the Pope's permission would be given eventually. Richard and Anne rode north, away from the king's court and troublesome George, to live at Middleham Castle in North Yorkshire.

Richard did a brilliant job of uniting most of the northern lords and keeping the warring Scots on their own side of the border. The city of York loved him for his fair treatment in law and his support in any business with the king – he negotiated a much smaller tax bill for them. Only two lords weren't happy with their new overlord, the Duke of Gloucester: Harry Percy, the Earl of Northumberland, who had always been quarrelling with Warwick too because he thought he should be in charge; and Lord Stanley who only ever did anything to suit himself and make certain the Stanley family came out on top.

Richard kept the king's peace in the north for ten years. During that time, in the summer of 1475, having been happily restored to his throne with assistance from Burgundy four years earlier, Edward IV decided it was time to show the Duke of Burgundy a little favour by helping him to invade France. It was all planned: every nobleman signed a contract stating how many knights, men-at-arms and archers he was expected to bring along; doctors and surgeons were signed up; provisions ordered and ships requisitioned to take men, horses, equipment and supplies across the Channel. Edward financed what he called his 'Enterprise of France' by raising 'benevolences'. He already had extra taxes granted by Parliament but that wasn't enough: benevolences were supposed to be additional voluntary contributions made by the better off merchants and citizens but, if they didn't pay up, the king demanded to know why not. The story goes that an elderly London widow made a donation and, when the good-looking king kissed her, she promptly doubled it. But not everyone was so enthusiastic, especially since Edward regarded benevolences as gifts, not loans to be repaid.

Richard had contracted to bring 10 knights, 100 lances and 1000 archers – the same as his brother George – but, in fact, Richard brought the largest contingent of any of the nobles, with men eager to serve under the Duke of Gloucester's White Boar badge. When Edward sailed to France in July, he took with him the biggest English army ever assembled to that date. But the campaign never happened. The Duke of Burgundy arrived late and said he had other, more important wars to fight so he and Edward quarrelled. The duke went off in a sulk, leaving the king to decide what he should do next. Edward chose to do a deal with the King of France. They would sign a peace treaty which was very favourable to the English: Edward's eldest daughter Elizabeth would marry the Dauphin (which never happened) and Edward would receive a big fat pension for life, so long as he withdrew his army from French soil without causing any trouble – which he did.

Richard was disgusted – all those taxes and benevolences wrung from the English... all for nothing. He called Edward's pension a French bribe – which it was. The people of England had paid up expecting glory, he said, but all they got was a dishonourable, cowardly retreat. When King Louis tried to bribe Edward's nobles to accept the treaty, they all took the money and gifts. Except Richard who was prepared to fight the war, alone. Edward gave his youngest brother a good talking-to, made him accept Louis's gifts – a huge cannon and Arab horses for his stud – and write a nice thank-you letter, which still exists, so we know what the presents were. Having obeyed but distanced himself from Edward's dealings, Richard sailed home, in good grace, for England, being giving a rapturous welcome for having refused to sign the treaty. When King Edward arrived in England, he had to pay cheer-leaders to make sure the boos and grumbles of the disgruntled tax-payers were drowned out during his journey back to London. Richard was flavour of the month.

In the autumn of 1477, Richard was shocked to hear the news that the king had had George arrested on a charge of treason and imprisoned him in the Tower of London. It seems George had taken the law into his own hands, accusing people of poisoning his wife Isabel and her baby, putting them on trial and executing them – something only the king was permitted to do. George had misbehaved before and the king had always forgiven him but this time it was different. Richard rushed to London for George's trial but seems to have been as mystified as everyone else by the proceedings. It was hardly a trial at all: neither side had lawyers. It was just George and the king shouting at each other, calling each other names and swapping insults. No one really knew what was going on but George was found guilty, all his titles and properties confiscated by the king and he was condemned to death.

Richard spent a miserable Christmas at court, trying to persuade Edward to forgive George yet again, horrified at the thought of one brother killing the other, while Parliament insisted the king should stop delaying the matter and sign the death warrant. History is a bit vague about what happened exactly but on 18th February 1478, George was found dead at the Tower of London, supposedly drowned in a barrel of Malmsey wine. Shakespeare blames Richard but he was the only one who tried to save George, not destroy him, and Richard blamed the queen and her brother for conniving to have George killed.

The third big occasion for Richard was in the summer of 1482. The Scots had been making nuisances of themselves, raiding northern England, stealing cattle and sheep, pillaging and laying waste what they couldn't take away. It was time to put an end to the problem. At that date, the town of Berwick-on-Tweed was an important Scottish port, well defended and often the base for the Scottish raiding parties. Richard besieged the town and won it back for England, moving the border with Scotland farther north. He then marched his army towards Edinburgh, unopposed. Maybe the

Scots were hopelessly disorganised or perhaps they were simply fed up with their useless king, James III, and his squabbling nobles.

Whatever the reason, Edinburgh opened its gates to Richard and welcomed him to the castle, giving him the keys to the city. King Edward was delighted with the success of the campaign, writing to the Pope personally, describing Richard as the best brother a king could want. He also granted Richard, for the future, the right to take and rule as much of Scotland he could manage; almost giving him permission to make himself a king.

But the following spring, on 9th April 1483, forty-year-old King Edward died suddenly and everything changed. Edward left instructions that Richard should be appointed Lord Protector to care for the new king, Edward V, who was just twelve, until he was old enough to rule alone. But neither young Prince Edward nor Richard were in London when the king died – the heir was at Ludlow Castle on the Welsh border, being tutored by his mother's brother, Earl Rivers, and Richard was somewhere in the wilds of the north. He didn't know his brother had died until Lord Hastings' message reached him, telling him to hurry to London before the queen's family caused trouble. Richard rode south but took time in York to have prayers said for his brother's soul and to have the northern lords swear allegiance to the new young king. More messages came from Hastings, begging him to come quickly as the queen was arranging for Earl Rivers and herself to take charge of the boy, with no mention of Richard as Lord Protector.

Richard journeyed south intending to meet the young king at Northampton, only to find that the king's party had already gone onto Stony Stratford, several miles closer to London. Earl Rivers joined Richard to tell him he had decided that two retinues would overcrowd Northampton. When the Duke of Buckingham arrived, during the night, Rivers was arrested. Next morning Richard and Buckingham rode into Stony Stratford early and, finding the king's party on the point of leaving for London, Richard acted swiftly, paying off and sending home the troops accompanying the young king. He then had Lord Grey, the young king's half-brother, and Sir Thomas Vaughan arrested, sending them and Earl Rivers north into captivity. Richard and Buckingham then carried on to London with the king.

Arriving in London, the new king was lodged in the palace of the Bishop of London, until Buckingham persuaded Richard to move him to the safety of the royal apartments at the Tower. The coronation was arranged for 24th June. Meantime, Lord Hastings changed his mind about supporting Richard and began to plot with the queen. Richard confronted him at a council meeting on Friday 13th June and ordered his execution. The rumour was that Hastings and others were plotting Richard's murder but only Hastings suffered the full penalty; the others, including Lord Stanley and John Morton, Bishop of Ely, were forgiven.

There was also startling news from the Bishop of Bath and Wells, that King Edward's marriage to Elizabeth Woodville-Grey was no marriage at all. Edward had already been troth-plight to another woman at the time, making his union illegal in the eyes of the Church. It seems likely the bishop had told George about this back in 1477 and that was why George had acted strangely, when he learned he was still Edward's rightful heir after all, and why the queen and her family were so determined he had to die. In view of this revelation, Richard was offered the crown by Parliament and accepted. He and Anne were crowned in Westminster Abbey on 6th July 1483.

Shortly after the coronation, the royal couple left London on a tour of the country. During their time away from London, the sons of Edward IV supposedly disappeared. Their fate is still a mystery.

Richard III, King of England

Richard and Anne were crowned on 6th July 1483, at a ceremony in Westminster Abbey that was attended by almost every nobleman, both Yorkist and Lancastrian. The common people, who must have been alarmed and confused by the events of the previous three weeks, seem to have accepted the outcome calmly and no one caused any disturbance of the ceremonies. Richard's men from York arrived late and were so shabby and ill-equipped that the Londoners thought they were a joke. But, on their way south, they had assisted with the executions of Rivers, Grey and Vaughan who had been tried before the Earl of Northumberland and con-demned for treason. Elizabeth Woodville's plots had lost her brother and son their heads; her other son his crown and reduced herself from Queen of England to Dame Elizabeth Grey, mistress of the late king.

Richard's first action was to take his seat on the King's Bench in Westminster Hall to give a stern speech to the Justices and Sergeants-at-law, ordering them to administer justice wisely and impartially to all, just as he was determined to show mercy and justice. Unfortunately, he would have to cope with too many men who knew the meaning of neither word.

He knew the difficulties he would face and the possibilities for mischief to be made out of the manner of his gaining the crown. Beneath the superficial rejoicing in London, he was aware of dangerous undercurrents. Recent events led to a vast amount of gossip, most of it harmless, but there were also more venomous rumours, inspired by Woodville supporters who, though their plots had failed, were still free to use their tongues. Whispers went round that the sons of Edward IV were in danger, persuading Elizabeth Woodville to remain in sanctuary at Westminster Abbey with her five daughters.

With London seeming calm, the new king made an awful mistake in setting out on a royal progress to his beloved north country only a fortnight after the coronation. No doubt, he was eager to involve the north, especially his young son and heir, in his dramatic change of fortune, wanting to celebrate with them. What he should have done was stay in the south, to confirm his position and deal with the dangers there. Instead, he travelled west to Reading, Oxford, Minster Lovell and the Cotswolds, as far as Gloucester.

It was there that the Duke of Buckingham, so prominent in recent affairs, left his royal cousin and rode to his castle of Brecknock, in Wales, taking with him the arch-schemer John Morton, Bishop of Ely — interesting company he must have been too. Meanwhile, Richard turned north to Warwick, Leicester and, eventually, York. The progress was a triumph; the king was greeted everywhere with enthusiasm by high and low alike. The Bishop of Saint David's, Dr Thomas Langton, was accompanying the king and wrote to the Prior of Christ Church, Canterbury saying:

The king contents the people where he goes best that ever did prince, for many a poor man that hath suffered wrong many days hath been relieved and helped by him and his commands in his progress. And in many great cities and towns were great sums of money given him which he hath refused. On my truth I liked never the conditions of any prince so well as his. God hath sent him to us for the weal of us all. (Christ Church Letters).

York welcomed its king with delight and wonderful pageants. At York Minster, Richard knighted his little son, Edward of Middleham, not yet ten years old, creating him Earl of Salisbury and Prince of Wales in a gorgeous ceremony, perhaps to make it up to the people of the north, his most loyal supporters, who had not been able to attend his coronation. Then, in the middle of September, he turned south again, reluctantly. He had reached Lincoln when news came that the southern counties were about to rise in rebellion and that the leader of the uprising was, unaccountably, his most trusted supporter, the Duke of Buckingham. No satisfactory explanation for Buckingham's astounding change of allegiance has ever come to light. He had, apparently, assisted Richard to the throne with such enthusiasm only three months before and been rewarded with the utmost generosity by a king who could hardly afford it. His change of heart was a mystery, bordering on madness.

The rebellion had been launched by people who demanded that the two young Princes in the Tower, Edward and Richard, Duke of York, should be freed. However, soon the rumours changed and stories spread that the children had been murdered, so the objective of the rebellion quietly changed to a scheme to bring Henry Tudor over from Brittany, put him on the throne and marry him to Elizabeth of York, eldest daughter of Edward IV and Elizabeth Woodville. The prime movers in this plot were John Morton (Buckingham's supposed prisoner), Margaret Beaufort, mother of Henry Tudor and currently wife of Lord Stanley, and Elizabeth Woodville who was involved to the extent of promising her daughter, Elizabeth, as the Tudor bride. It must have been Morton who persuaded Buckingham to be the figurehead of the rebellion but quite how he got the arrogant duke to support a Tudor claim to the throne, when the duke had a much better claim himself, is impossible to understand. There must have been empty promises made and, perhaps, the future disposal of Buckingham planned in advance. Buckingham's only possible motive was that his family had always been supporters of the House of Lancaster and he was simply reverting to type, but then nothing was ever 'simple' when the duke was involved.

Bishop Morton was, first and last, interested only in his own advancement and had probably imagined a rosy future as chief advisor during the minority of a Woodville king. No chance of that with Richard of Gloucester at the helm though so, when the Woodville hopes came to nothing, Morton returned to his old allegiance with Henry Tudor as Lancaster's heir: he couldn't have chosen a better master to suit himself. As for Margaret Beaufort, her motive was simple: to set her only son on the throne of England. But the revolt came to nothing. His own incompetence, combined with floods that prevented him from crossing the River Severn, proved Buckingham's downfall. Henry Tudor, cruising in the Channel with a few ships, declined to join the debacle as Buckingham was captured, tried for high treason at Salisbury, and executed. Margaret Beaufort's life was spared, on condition her husband, Lord Stanley, should be responsible for her good behaviour. Morton escaped abroad to join Henry Tudor. Richard was too lenient towards the rebels: there were very few executions and he restored the felons' forfeited estates to their heirs in some cases. The rumours about the Princes in the Tower faded away in England, though they persisted on the continent, nurtured by Bishop Morton for the benefit of his new protégé, Henry Tudor.

Richard's Parliament

In January 1484, Richard held his first and only Parliament, put off from the previous autumn because of Buckingham's rebellion. His Parliament passed laws that forced his later, ardent critic, Francis Bacon, to admit that he was 'a good law maker for the ease and solace of the common people'. Of primary importance to the king himself was the confirmation of his title in the *Titulus Regius* act. This set out the fact that the pre-contract of marriage between Edward IV and Lady Eleanor Butler, and the subsequent clandestine marriage between Edward and Elizabeth Woodville, made Edward V, his brother and sisters illegitimate under Church law. Richard's title and that of his heirs now received the full authority of the Statute Book.

Other laws were passed which must have pleased the common folk: Edward IV's favourite method of collecting money as 'free gifts' from his subjects, known as 'benevolences' and hated by all as a tax by any other name, was made illegal. Another law instructed that people arrested on suspicion of a crime should be allowed bail and that their goods should not be seized before conviction. This had been a lord's method for getting his hands on the desirable property of an innocent tenant: have him arrested on suspicion, seize his goods, and then, when he is found innocent and released, well... possession is nine tenths of the law, so hard luck on the tenant! Then there were a number of acts dealing with the import of goods from abroad, imposing restrictions and customs duties with the aim of making home-produced goods more competitive. These would have pleased the English craftsmen rather than the wealthy merchants but Richard was also concerned for the improvement of education in the country. With this in mind, he personally advised Parliament to exempt books from these acts, since most books were still printed abroad, and to allow foreigners, practicing any and all aspects of book production and trade, to live and work freely in England.

These reforms benefited Richard's humbler subjects but weren't popular with the nobles, the wealthy merchants and those in authority whose interests suffered, losing Richard a lot of support later on. Parliament also passed the acts of attainder against those who had been active in the recent rebellion: that was to be expected. But here Richard made another mistake that was to cost him the support of the majority of noblemen in the south of England — he parceled out the rebels' lands to his northern supporters, bringing in too many men who were regarded as foreigners by the local communities. Known as 'the planting of the Northerners', far from calming things down in the south, the king's men were resented, making the area a hotbed of discontent for the future.

The Road to Bosworth Field

In February 1484, Elizabeth Woodville left sanctuary and placed herself and her daughters under Richard's protection, while he made a solemn promise that he would respect their persons and provide suitably for their futures as his kinswomen. It isn't surprising that Elizabeth should require such a promise, considering her own activities during the past year and her scheming with Margaret Beaufort and Henry Tudor. At a later date, Elizabeth wrote to her only remaining son from her first marriage, the Marquis of Dorset, hiding out in France, telling him to return to England where the king would treat him well. Dorset set out to obey her instructions but was forcibly prevented from leaving France by Henry Tudor's henchmen.

In April 1484, Richard suffered a devastating, and eventually fatal, blow in the sudden death of his only legitimate son, Edward, Prince of Wales, at Middleham.

The significance of this loss cannot be over-stated. Richard seems to have been a devoted father and all his personal hopes had been centred on this child. More than that, the future of the Yorkist dynasty, essential to the peace of the country and the stability of his throne, died with the boy. The queen was inconsolable too, knowing her poor health made it impossible she should give her husband another child. This meant the country was once again faced with the hazards of a disputed succession and, recalling a century of civil unrest for this same cause, people had good reason for renewed misgivings. Richard himself was still quite popular but the prospect of a childless king undermined his subjects' faith in the future.

The death of the Prince of Wales heralded another outbreak of rumours concerning the sons of Edward IV, for the idea of divine retribution was firmly fixed in medieval minds. As before, the rumours seem to have come from France. Once again, Henry Tudor saw an opportunity as the result of Richard's loss. He had sworn to marry Elizabeth, the undoubted daughter of Edward IV, whether legitimate or not, and so unite the Lancastrian and Yorkist factions. He could now advertise himself as the potential founder of a new dynasty which might well appeal to Richard's anxious subjects whose chief concern was for a peaceful future. There was a lot of coming and going of Henry's agents and the rumours grew and multiplied.

In March 1485, as if he didn't have problems enough, Queen Anne also died. Richard wept openly at her funeral but more rumours started immediately, to the effect that the king had poisoned his wife in order to marry his niece, Elizabeth. Richard was obliged to issue a public denial of this story which had offended many of his people. How his position could have been improved by marrying his brother's illegitimate daughter is hard to see, except that it might have given him the chance of producing a new heir, but then there were plenty of potential foreign brides more suitable. The argument that he would marry her simply to deprive Henry Tudor of his selected bride doesn't stand up either, as it seems Richard was proposing her marriage to the Earl of Desmond at the time, but it was just another slander to heap upon the unfortunate king.

Several of the disgruntled nobles began a treasonable correspondence with Henry, chief among them his stepfather, Lord Stanley, his step-uncle, Sir William Stanley, and the Earl of Northumberland. Richard, always slow to recognise treachery among those he believed to be his friends, remained ignorant of the treason that surrounded him until the very end, though he understood, by this time, that Henry would make a bid for the throne. Richard even made Lord Stanley and his son, Lord Strange, Commissioners of Array for Wales, while Northumberland was all-powerful in the north.

Throughout his reign, Richard had been strapped for cash, the Woodvilles having made away with the late king's treasury and Richard himself having rewarded his friends most generously, in some cases remitting the property forfeited by his enemies to their relatives. He had refused the lavish gifts pressed on him by towns and cities during his progresses, saying he would rather have their loyalty than their money but, now the realm was threatened with invasion, he had to pay for its defence somehow. He had outlawed his brother's method of the hated benevolences and would not use them, even as a last resort, so he sent messages to his wealthier subjects, asking for loans for which he gave security and the promise of repayment at specified dates. With the money, he equipped an army and set up his headquarters at Nottingham, conveniently central in the kingdom so as to have the shortest route to intercept the invader, wherever he might come ashore.

Henry Tudor landed at Milford Haven on 7th August 1485, with a force composed of foreign mercenaries, the remnants of the Lancastrian party and the sweeping from French gaols, paid for by his mother, Margaret Beaufort, and the Regent of France, Anne de Beaujeu, sister to the new young king, Charles VIII. Sir William Stanley openly supported the rebels and was proclaimed a traitor. Lord Stanley, professing loyalty to Richard, secretly promised support to his stepson. The two armies met near Market Bosworth in Leicestershire on Monday 22nd August. The battle lasted barely two hours, both Stanleys throwing their forces into the fight on Henry's side, while Northumberland, who commanded the king's reserves, refused to take part in the battle at all. Richard, seeing himself betrayed on all sides, made a desperate bid to retrieve the day, charging at the head of a small band of faithful knights into the heart of the enemy ranks. He was so nearly successful in his aim to reach the Tudor, killing the enemy's standard bearer and unhorsing his bodyguard before he was killed, fighting bravely, surrounded by his enemies.

After the battle, his body was stripped naked and thrown across the back of a packhorse for the journey to Leicester. There he was exposed to the insults of the mob for two days, after which he was buried by the brothers in the church of the Grey Friars. Richard was deeply mourned, especially in the north where he was best known. His downfall had been brought about by a combination of adverse circumstances, the disloyalty of three discontented nobles and one scheming woman. Entirely loyal himself, he was unable to recognise treachery in others or to deal with it with sufficient ruthlessness when it became obvious. His leniency towards traitors was unusual and fatal, since it eventually cost him his crown.

Pretenders to the Tudor throne

In January 1486, Henry had wed Elizabeth of York but, in order to do so, he had been forced to get Parliament to legitimise her. But here was a dilemma – if Elizabeth was declared legitimate, then so were her brothers, the Princes in the Tower. If they were still alive, they could now claim to be the legitimate heirs to the throne of England. You can see why anyone claiming to be one of those boys was such a worry to King Henry on his newly-won throne.

As Jeremy Potter says in his introduction to his book: *Pretenders*; 'They may be imposters or they may be princes. Plausibility is the overriding qualification: it alone can attract a following and recognition'.

Perkin Warbeck

Both Lambert Simnel and Perkin Warbeck met this criterion in the late 1480s and 1490s, as very plausible pretenders to the throne of England in the early years of the reign of King Henry VII, a man who understood the concept well, having been a 'pretender' himself to the throne of King Richard before he met with success at the battle of Bosworth in 1485.

Let's begin with Lambert Simnel, as history has come to know him. Henry VII's biographer writes that the boy was commonly born, whether the son of a baker or cobbler and adds that he was from Oxford. However obscure his origins, Lambert Simnel, under the guidance of a priest, Richard Symonds, found his way to Ireland and, in the spring of 1487, he became the focus of rebellion for a group of diehard Yorkists wishing to depose Henry VII. According to Tudor sources, the boy claimed to be the young Earl of Warwick whom Henry VII had incarcerated in the Tower of London since the battle of Bosworth, two years before. So it would seem simply a matter of producing the earl from his prison cell and showing him to the populace, demonstrating the truth and refuting the claims of the Yorkists in Ireland.

This is exactly what Henry did, except his actions didn't undo the Yorkists' cause as he had hoped. Rumours abounded that the true Earl of Warwick *was* in Ireland and that the boy Henry paraded through the streets of London was the imposter. Recently, Gordon Smith has suggested another alternative: that Henry *did* produce the true Earl of Warwick but the lad in Ireland was never claiming to be that young man. Instead, he was the elder son of King Edward IV and therefore the rightful King of England, now that Henry had legitimised the offspring of King Edward. So it seems possible the Tudor government was using Warwick to distract attention from the activities in Ireland and the name 'Lambert Simnel' was an alias invented by the Tudors who dared not suggest the lad's true identity.

Edward IV

For one thing, the Yorkists never said the boy in Ireland was Lambert Simnel, nor that he was the Earl of Warwick – all of that was the Tudor's invention. The Yorkists actually had the boy crowned as King Edward – no regnal number was given – but the seal they used for his writs and proclamations was that of Edward V, the elder of the Princes in the Tower. Now the solemn act of coronation in the Middle Ages was seen as God giving his approval to the new monarch. To crown a baker's boy would be incredibly insulting to God and to the people over whom he was to reign.

The Yorkists would never have committed such a blasphemy, especially as the Earl of Lincoln, designated as Richard III's heir when the little princes were still officially illegitimate, was right there at the coronation, handy if they needed a suitable candidate for the crown. Yet he fully supported the new king, so was the boy truly young Edward V?

In Christchurch Cathedral, Dublin, the Archbishop of Dublin presided, assisted by the Bishops of Meath, Kildare and Cloyne. An impressive array of Anglo-Irish lords and Yorkist notables from England completed the distinguished assembly for the coronation on 24th May 1487. It is usually assumed that the lad was proclaimed Edward VI but, in fact, only the York Civic Records give him this designation of 'the Sixth'. Coins minted in Ireland during the rebellion are inscribed simply: Edwardvs, as are documents issued there as early as 13th August 1486.

Whoever he was, the activities of the Yorkists in Ireland had to be taken seriously and certainly posed a threat to Henry's new dynasty, for there were no doubts concerning the true origins and intentions of the leaders: John de la Pole, Earl of Lincoln, and Francis, Viscount Lovell of Tichmarsh: formerly Richard's Lord Chamberlain. The Irish lords also gave their support, willing to provide men for an invasion of England.

They were not the only ones eager to assist either: the dowager Duchess of Burgundy, Margaret of York, sister to both Edward IV and Richard III, was certainly involved in the Lambert Simnel affair and persuaded her son-in-law Maximillian, King of the Romans, to provide money, mercenaries and equipment, all of which were sent to Ireland, to join the Yorkist force assembling there.

Whatever the true identity of the lad, the army raised in his name sailed on 4th June 1487 and was brought across the Irish Sea 'by a great navy with a multitude of strangers' to land near Broughton-in-Furness, a remote part of the Lancashire coast. With the Earl of Lincoln leading the host, they marched eastwards across the Pennines, trusting men to flock to their banner. They must have been sadly dismayed by the apathetic response which was not at all what they had hoped for. Never the less, Lincoln, undeterred and realising he must act before his army became too demoralised, marched south, towards Newark. Henry Tudor was waiting for them, his own army impressively arrayed and ready to face the ill-assorted foreigners who were the bulk of the Pretender's little army: a mixture of disciplined German mercenaries and Irish peasants armed with little more than their own fierce enthusiasm for a fight, along with a few Yorkist veterans.

The two armies engaged on 16th June by the village of East Stoke on the River Trent, just south west of Newark, in Nottinghamshire. The German mercenaries faced Henry's vanguard which was lead by the Lancastrian stalwart, John de Vere, Earl of Oxford, who had fought so doggedly at Bosworth two years before. Henry's army had cannon and long bows whereas the rebels' only artillery may have been a few arquebuses (hand guns), the Germans being armed with cross-bows in the main. With the Irish having a few bowmen but the rest almost all naked and unarmed, it was an uneven and bloody fight, the Pretender's army was cut down and wholesale slaughter followed. Despite King Henry's wish that the Earl of Lincoln should be taken alive, in order that he might reveal the facts behind the conspiracy, he was slain in the field, and Viscount Lovell disappeared.

As for young King Edward, he reverted to his former identity, true or otherwise, as Lambert Simnel and was taken into King Henry's own household as a turnspit in the kitchens, later to rise to the position of falconer in the royal mews. In either humble position, Henry intended to humiliate the now-harmless young Pretender and to display him as a warning to any future would-be claimants to his throne, that a life of ignominy was the best they might achieve. However, Gordon Smith suggests it was now that the Tudors substituted a 'Lambert Simnel' for the real Edward V, who may either have died in battle or been killed afterwards on Henry's orders. This 'Lambert' was the boy who entered the king's service as a scullion and passed his days in safe, honest, if lowly, servitude.

King Henry's dismay at the death of the Earl of Lincoln in the battle is understandable, since much of the reasoning behind the rebellion was obscure even at the time. Lincoln would have been able to reveal the true identity of Lambert Simnel, if Henry did not know it already which, possibly, he didn't. If he could have discovered what really had happened to the nephews of King Richard III, things would have been much easier for the Tudor king in the following decade. That he was not certain of the little princes' fate becomes apparent as we turn to the career of a more troublesome Pretender, Perkin Warbeck, who began his meteoric rise to fame in 1491, in the town of Cork, in Ireland.

As for his earlier career, like Lambert Simnel before him, he has two possible histories, depending on whether he was the Yorkist prince he claimed to be, or the son of a Tournai boatman, as Tudor sources declared was the case. According to George Buck, writing in Stuart times, the Tudor historians were agreed on one point:

The man (say they) commonly called Perkin Warbeck was as well with the Princes, as with the people, English and forraigne, held to be the younger Son of Edward the fourth, and that the deaths of the young King Edward

and of Richard his brother, had come so far in question,
as some are yet in doubt whether they were destroyed
or no, in the dayes of King Richard; By which it appeares
they were thought to be living after his death.

Buck also tells of the possibility that the princes
were 'set safe on shore beyond Seas'. If this was so,
it would be one explanation of an English prince's
Burgundian childhood. Diana Kleyn goes further in
this vein as to name the princes' possible saviours,
who took them 'beyond Seas', as Sir James Tyrell and
Sir Edward Brampton, with all the necessary supporting arguments. As further backing, we have the young
man's letter to Queen Isabella of Spain but against it
we have his later confession, whilst in Tudor captivity,
in which he reveals his Warbeck parentage and a letter
written to his 'mother' during the same period.

Whatever the truth of his origins, Perkin Warbeck
appeared in Cork in the autumn of 1491, splendidly
attired in the silks which his master, Pierre-Jean Meno,
a Breton merchant, desired to sell. Clad in this way,
as the Tudor sources relate, so fine did he look that,
by his appearance alone, John Atwater and others declared he must be the illegitimate son of King Richard
III. The lad denied this on oath but, eventually, it was
decided that either he was, or he should impersonate,
Richard, Duke of York, the younger of the two Princes
in the Tower.

The new Pretender started to gather quite a following and the heads of state throughout Europe began to take notice of the activities of this young man. In March 1492, he was at the French court where the King of France honoured him and gave him a bodyguard. He was joined in France by about a hundred dissident Yorkists.

With Charles VIII of France giving the Pretender support so openly, the situation became very tense to the point where, in the autumn of 1492, Henry Tudor declared war against the French. However, Henry's intentions were more devious than belligerent. Peace with France was concluded with the Treaty of Etaples inNovember, the Tudor king given money and promises that France would not support 'the enemies of England', i.e. Perkin Warbeck.

But for Henry this solved nothing. Perkin Warbeck and his growing band of Yorkist adherents simply moved on to the court of Burgundy and this affair, unlike that of Lambert Simnel, was achieving international significance: a far greater threat to Henry's throne. When the Emperor Frederic III died the following year, the Pretender travelled with the Duke of Saxony to Vienna, to attend the funeral. There, he was given full honours as King Richard IV of England. On first seeing the young man who claimed to be her nephew, Margaret of York, dowager Duchess of Burgundy, declared that she had doubts but, when she subjected him to close questioning, 'he never faltered nor made a mistake in his knowledge of the court of King Edward'. She was convinced of the truth of his claim and owned him her own nephew.

Other Yorkists observed the lad closely, noting 'such private marks as hee had bin knawne by from his Cradle... by his Face Countenance, Lineaments and all tokens familiarly and privately knowne to them'. Not only that, but he behaved with the grace and manners of a prince, speaking English perfectly. If what George Buck tells us was the truth, there seems little doubt that this young man was the genuine prince and certainly his fellow Yorkists found themselves 'so well satisfied, and were so confirmed that they wrote to the Lord Fitzwater, to Sir Symon Mountford and others... the full account of what they had observed'.

So the Pretender was now developing quite a following in England too, even among men of the Church, like William Worsley, the Dean of St Paul's and Abbot Sant of Abingdon in Oxfordshire. However, with plans for a summer invasion of England well underway in Burgundy, things went badly wrong for the Pretender: Sir Robert Clifford suddenly left the Yorkist enclave and returned to the Tudor court where he revealed to King Henry the names of the most important conspirators still on English soil. Quite how much 'persuasion' had to be used on Clifford in order to gain this information is debatable; it seems probable he was an *agent provocateur* all the time. At the end of January 1495, Sir Simon Mountford and others were arrested and beheaded, others were hanged at Tyburn. Lord FitzWalter was spared and imprisoned in Calais; the churchmen were pardoned but heavily fined.

With his support in England now devastated, the chances of a successful invasion were greatly reduced but the Pretender made the attempt, all the same. On 3rd July 1495, about 300 men landed on Deal beach in Kent and set up three standards there but that was the height of their achievement. The locals kept the beleaguered band of rebels at bay, hemming them in on the beach until Sir John Peche, the Sheriff of Kent, arrived with his militia. Although his captains and others were taken prisoner, the Pretender hadn't disembarked and sailed away with his little flotilla to fight another day.

Aware that any attempt at invading England would be certain to find favour with Scotland, he sailed north and was soon comfortably provided for at the court of James IV, the young King of Scots, with an allowance for clothes, servants and horses and even the financial backing to stage another invasion of England. Whatever doubts anyone else may have had about the young man's true identity, King James had none, treating Perkin Warbeck as a friend, a cousin and an equal. He allowed him to marry into the Scots royal family giving him the hand of the Lady Catherine Gordon and paying for the wedding out of the Scottish Treasury.

The invasion across the border into English territory began on 21st September 1496, the army marching under the colours of both Scotland and Yorkist England. King James set about conducting the war in the usual Scottish fashion of burning, looting and pillaging but the Pretender realised this treatment of the English people, amongst whom he wished to gain loyal support, could not fail to turn them against him. This proved to be the case and the enterprise was abandoned, much to King James's chagrin and the Pretender's deep disappointment. He remained in Scotland at King James's expense for another year but, eventually, it became politic for him to leave.

He and his wife, styled the Duke and Duchess of York, sailed away in a ship, *The Cuckoo*, once more bound for Ireland. Their journey was far from uneventful but they eventually made landfall in Cornwall, at Whitesand Bay in September 1497. The men of Cornwall were already in a state of revolt, having marched on London and been routed at Blackheath by the royal army back in June. When the Pretender (having left the duchess safe on St Michael's Mount) raised his standard at Bodmin, proclaiming himself as King Richard IV, men flocked to his banner. With 3000-4000 Cornish men, he besieged Exeter, without success. When he reached Taunton, he found himself facing the royal army. Henry Tudor promised him a pardon if he surrendered but, rightly not trusting Henry's word, at dawn the following day the standard of Richard IV had disappeared and the man along with it. Leaderless now, the brave little Cornish army gave up. Henry sent men to St Michael's Mount to retrieve the duchess and treated her well.

The Pretender was found at Beaulieu Abbey in Hampshire and taken back to Taunton where he appeared before King Henry on 5th October 1497. He was forced to submit and to declare that his real name was Piers Osbeck of Tournai. He was made to write a lengthy confession, detailing his life and travels but how much is truth and how much Tudor propaganda is open to debate. The Pretender was in London by the end of November, lead through Cheapside and Cornhill to the Tower, and then back again, through Candlewick Street to Westminster, exposed to taunts and humiliation.

From the international point of view, Perkin Warbeck was now an embarrassment to King Henry and a way had to be found of bringing the problem to a tidy conclusion. Having made an unsuccessful attempt to escape from the palace at Richmond, the Pretender was kept under guard at the Tower of London. Here, after a humiliating session in the stocks, he was incarcerated close to his 'cousin', the unfortunate Earl of Warwick, and Henry had found the means to rid himself of both troublesome Yorkist princes. Their gaolers were to encourage the two young cousins to indulge in a treasonable correspondence with each other, each trying to cheer the other with talk about escaping from the Tower. The gaolers promptly showed the letters to Henry.

On 16th November 1499, the Pretender was arraigned on a charge of high treason and on the 23rd November he was drawn on a hurdle to Tyburn. On the scaffold, he was made to read aloud his confession once again before meeting the death of a common felon: he was hanged, drawn and quartered. The Earl of Warwick had been tried the day before, also for high treason. His uncompassionate peers found him guilty, although he was permitted to suffer the death of a nobleman: he was beheaded. The heads of both young men were set on London Bridge; their bodies buried in the cemetery of the Augustinian Friars in London.

In the case of both Pretenders, Henry Tudor had gone to great lengths to make light of the threat to his throne. But the amount of diplomatic activity, the fact that he signed the Treaty of Etaples to remove Perkin Warbeck from the hands of the King of France, proves otherwise. Another grave concern of Henry's must have been the extent of the Pretenders' support in England, particularly in 1495, when noblemen and abbots, even his own Lord Chamberlain were found to be plotting his downfall. What this proves is that not only Henry Tudor but important people throughout the kingdom, and Europe, believed that one or possibly both, of King Edward's sons had lived beyond the reign of Richard III.

The guilt or innocence of Richard III regarding the prince's murders is unlikely ever to be proven, one way or the other. Until recently, it is this very mystery that has made the last Plantagenet king so famous. Books, whether academic tomes, popular illustrated coffee table editions or romantic historical novels, will be produced for years to come, each with their own particular slant on Richard as either 'England's Black Legend', a cross between Saint George and Sir Galahad, or something in between. Further evidence that the princes survived Richard's reign has now come to light through the research undertaken for the 'The Missing Princes Project' and published in November 2023.

For myself, I see him as a man of his time: hopeful, fallible, trying to make the best of a tricky situation. As you have heard, I don't believe he murdered his nephews but then I also don't think anyone else did either, at least until Henry VII had 'Perkin Warbeck' executed in 1499. I hope I have supplied you with plenty of food for thought and ideas for discussion on this subject. Whether you agree with my findings or not is up to you: but that is the nature of this controversial king, Richard III.

The Mystery of the Princes

Of all the crimes attributed to Richard III, none causes more debate and emotion than that of his alleged murder of Edward V and Richard, Duke of York: 'The Princes in the Tower'. It is impossible to prove the case either way. To the Tudor myth-makers, it was the climax of Richard's villainy. Based on rumours that circulated in England since the summer of 1483, people began to say positively that Richard had murdered them. John Rous, writing shortly after Richard's death, says 'he ascended the throne of the slaughtered children', but does not expand on this.

Henry VII made his personal contribution to the myth when he had the story spread that Sir James Tyrell had 'confessed' to murdering the princes on Richard's orders. This confession was published soon after Tyrell's execution in 1502. Henry had his own reasons for claiming this so long after the event — the future of the Tudor line depended on the heir marrying a princess. But no foreign king wanted his daughter wed to a Tudor if a 'true King of England' was going to appear suddenly. Henry VII needed to put an end to any idea that the Princes in the Tower had survived. Tyrell's supposed 'confession' became the source for all the subsequent detailed accounts of Richard's murder of his nephews.

It was Polydore Vergil and Thomas More who built up the rumours and accusations. Thomas More, in particular, gives elaborate details of the murder. He wrote '...so began he with most piteous and wicked [deaths]; I mean the lamentable murder of his innocent nephews, the young King and his tender brother.' There follows the familiar story of Tyrell and his henchmen, Dighton and Forest, smothering the princes with pillows. Both Vergil and More reported that this was only one of a number of explanations for the princes' disappearance. The mid-16th century chroniclers, Hall and Holinshead, follow Sir Thomas More while Shakespeare creates the supremely villainous Richard casually arranging the murders and Tyrell reporting the details of their deaths over supper.

Rumours that Richard had done away with the princes were inevitable in the circumstances of his accession. In the 15th century, people tended to believe whatever they were told, mainly for want of any other sources of information. The Croyland Chronicle reported that, after Richard's coronation, there began a movement to free the princes '...public proclamation having been made that Henry, Duke of Buckingham.... being repentant of what had been done, would be captain in chief of this affair, a rumour arose that King Edward's sons, by some unknown manner of violent destruction, had met their fate.' The chronicler, who was otherwise well informed, does not confirm the rumour. The French Chancellor, Guillaume de Rochefort, in a speech to the Estates General in January 1484, said the English Crown had '...been transferred to their murderer by the favour of the people.' This was most likely meant as a warning to the French people themselves since, at the time, they were ruled by a king in his minority with his elder sister as regent.

It has been suggested that murdering his nephews would have been out of character for Richard III. P.M. Kendall wrote: *'Despite the legend, Richard's record does not reveal an unprincipled and bloodthirsty tyrant. He spared traitors like Morton and Stanley after a conspiracy which could have cost him his life ... this does not suggest the kind of man who would kill the young sons of a brother to whom he had been unswervingly loyal.'* However, others argue that political necessity and survival create their own reasons.

The fate of another nephew of Richard provides a clue. Clarence's son, Edward, Earl of Warwick, had a better claim than Richard to the throne, but for his father's attainder. Richard treated him kindly, at one time making him his heir. Henry VII, on the other hand, imprisoned him in the Tower and later had him executed. Other factors to remember include the behaviour of Elizabeth Woodville, mother of the princes, during Richard's reign and her subsequent reaction to the Lambert Simnel rebellion, which she supported. And the doubts in many people's minds, caused by the arrival of the various pretenders, claiming to be one or other of the princes during the reign of Henry VII, shows that no one was certain they had died. Despite all the theories, the questions of motive, the debates over character, we are still as far away as ever from finding out what really did happen to the sons of Edward IV. All we know is that they were last seen at the Tower in 1483. There are no facts sufficient to find Richard, or any of the other suspects, guilty.

The two most likely candidates for the murder of the princes, after Richard, are Henry VII and the Duke of Buckingham. In both cases the evidence is circumstantial rather than factual. Henry certainly had motive and opportunity, if the boys were still alive in captivity after Bosworth and his own claim would have been ruined by their continued existence. Buckingham had opportunity during 1483, when he had access to the Tower as Constable of England. His behaviour and subsequent rebellion raise questions about his involvement with their fate. But we are no better off than the Italian visitor, Dominic Mancini, when he wrote over 500 year ago: 'Whether, however, he (the young King Edward V) has been done away with and by what manner of death, so far I have not at all discovered'.

But the mystery of what happened to the Princes in the Tower may finally have been solved by Philippa Langley's 'The Missing Princes Project'. Newly discovered documents have now been revealed and it seems both Pretenders to the Tudor throne, ignominiously named as Lambert Simnel, a baker's boy, and Perkin Warbeck, son of a Tournai boatman, *were* who they claimed to be: the sons of King Edward IV. According to these discoveries, Richard III was not a murderer of innocent princes. Both were smuggled out of the country for their own safety: the elder boy, Edward, probably to Jersey in the Channel Islands; the younger, Richard, to France and both lived to, literally, fight another day.

The Bones in The Tower

In July 1674, workmen in the Tower of London, dig-
ging under the stairs leading from the King's Lodgings
to the Chapel in the White Tower, found the skeletons
of two children. Since the place of discovery coincided
with Thomas More's account of the disposal of the
bodies of the princes, and according to a contemporary eye-witness, scraps of velvet were found with the
bones, they were assumed to be those of Edward V
and Richard, Duke of York. On Charles II's orders they
were deposited in a marble urn in Henry VII's Chapel,
Westminster Abbey. One problem with thinking the
discovery of the bones fits well with More's story is
that, in the next paragraph, More tells how Richard, his
conscience stricken, has the bodies dug up again and
buried in holy ground, so they weren't under the stairs
any longer, anyway.

In July 1933, the urn was opened in an attempt to determine whether the bones could be those of the princes. The remains were examined by Professor Wright of the Royal College of Surgeons and Dr George Northcroft, a dental surgeon, but not by an anthropologist, a mediaeval archaeologist or a forensic scientist. They agreed the bones were those of a child aged between twelve and thirteen and a younger child aged between nine and eleven. Certain peculiar features about the bones suggested a close family relationship, while the elder child seemed to have suffered from a disease in the jaw which would have affected its general health. There was also a stain on the skull which, Wright claimed though could not prove, was a bloodstain. Their conclusion was that the bones were those of King Edward V and his brother and were compatible with their deaths in the summer of 1483, when Edward was twelve years and nine months old and Richard was about to celebrate his tenth birthday.

Subsequently, experts have cast doubt on these conclusions, believing the anatomical evidence for the ages of the children and for death by smothering, as indicated by the stain on the skull, to be unsound, although the dental evidence is generally stronger. Scientific methods of dating bones have advanced so much since 1933 and the differences in development between medieval and modern children may be helped by the discovery in 1964 of the coffin and remains of

Anne Mowbray, child-wife of Richard of York, whose age and date of death are known. This gives a direct contemporary parallel to judge the age and development of the controversial skeletons. Alongside this we now have CAT scans, DNA testing and great advances in forensic pathology but, despite a request by the Richard III Society for a chance to re-examine the bones from the urn, the Dean of Westminster has refused, to date, to allow a further disturbance of them in their current resting place.

The King in the
Car Park

Contemporary historical sources say that, after the battle of Bosworth, the body of Richard III was put on public view in Leicester, so everyone could be certain he was dead, then it was interred in the choir of the Grey Friars Church. At the Reformation, the friary was demolished and tradition had it that Richard's remains were thrown in the River Soar. But were they?

In 1612, fifty years after the dissolution, the Rev Christopher Wren (the father of the architect Christopher Wren) recorded that Leicester Alderman Robert Herrick '...had a handsome stone pillar in his garden, marking the spot where the body of King Richard III lay.' His garden was marked on old maps of Leicester, within the area of the modern city still known as The Grey Friars. Amazingly, after 500 years of development and change, only parts of the garden had been built on; the remaining spaces were now used by the city council as car parks. The University of Leicester Archaeological Service (ULAS) had already done some excavation work in the area, looking for the church in nearby Grey Friars Street, to the south of Herrick's Garden. They had only found a small part of a stone coffin lid but no church; the church was elsewhere.

Philippa Langley and John Ashdown-Hill, both members of the Richard III Society, had been research- ing the subject individually for years. After tireless campaigning by Philippa a project was created and the society asked to subscribe to a fund to help pay for an archaeological excavation.

The dig began in late August 2012 in the car park a little way from Leicester Cathedral. Although a great deal of research had been done in the hope of finding the site of the medieval Church of the Grey Friars and this seemed to be the place, geo-physics examination had been of little help because water-mains, gas pipes, electricity and communication cables all ran beneath the car park.

A spot was chosen for the first trench where the letter 'R' for 'Reserved' marked one of the parking bays. The first noteworthy discovery was a human left leg bone at the edge of the trench – a good find but not surprising when excavating around a church. This was found approximately 5m from the north end of the trench, about 1.5m below modern ground level. Care- ful examination revealed a parallel right leg, indicating an undisturbed burial (pleasing but again only to be expected). The remains were noted and covered to protect them from the weather until more was known about where they were located in relation to the friary. Lead archaeologist, Richard Buckley, joked that he'd 'eat his hat if it was Richard III'.

The skeleton had been shoved into the grave which was too small for it but walls and high quality floor tiles found close by proved the burial was in the choir, close to the altar, so it had to be an important person. Yet there was no sign that there had ever been a coffin, or even a shroud, and the way the arms lay, wrists together on the pelvis, suggested the hands had been tied together in front of the body when it went into the grave. The feet were missing but this was due to the later building of a Victorian outside loo – it was just luck that it hadn't disturbed the rest of the skeleton. On 12th September the University of Leicester announced that 'a skeleton' had been found.

A Royal Skeleton?

This would hardly have been worth a news conference if they hadn't had some idea that it might be *the* skeleton. Was the lead archaeologist going to have to 'eat his hat' after all? What were the chances that this was the last Plantagenet king and what made it seem likely? As the skeleton was excavated by Jo Appleby, the osteo-archaeologist couldn't miss the obvious bend in the spine – the body had been severely affected by scoliosis. When the bones were boxed, Philippa had leapt to conclusions and asked Jo to drape the box in a medieval royal standard. This was perverse – the society has generally maintained that Richard's hunchback was just so much Tudor propaganda but Philippa, though shocked, seemed very keen to accept that the scoliosis proved it was the king's skeleton. Jo refused to treat the remains as 'royalty' as they were still unidentified.

Other factors pointed to a violent death in battle: numerous minor wounds show on the bones – there were probably more that were only inflicted on soft tissue and haven't left any trace – and a deep penetration wound to the top of the skull and two slices hacked from the back of the skull, both deep enough to have exposed the brain. Any of these three injuries would have been fatal; none show even the first stages of healing, so all were inflicted around the time of death. What was thought to be an arrowhead in the back turned out to be an old iron nail; nothing to do with the remains.

Despite the evidence that the body had been killed in battle, there did seem to be some reason to think these were the bones of a woman. They were slim and gracile and the pelvic arch – the most usual way of telling a male skeleton from a female – was edging towards the more feminine shape. The face had been left pretty much intact and it too had delicate brow arches, whereas those in a male skeleton are often, though not always, more pronounced. But the skeleton would have stood about 5' 9" if it had been able to stand straight. How much the scoliosis would have affected the height is hard to judge. It may even be the case that shoving the body into a too-short grave has exaggerated the curvature in death.

We know – if it was Richard – that he wore plate armour and was a doughty warrior, veteran of at least two pitched battles. Hard to credit if he was greatly deformed in overall body shape. A modern sufferer from a similar type and degree of scoliosis appeared severely twisted when undressed but, when clothed, it was not apparent unless you knew to look for it. Maybe that is why only the Tudor chroniclers mention it, the condition only becoming common knowledge after his corpse was stripped of its armour following the battle.

Carbon Dating

Back to the facts: carbon dating was done on a sample of bone – it could have dated to any time between the friary's foundation in the thirteenth century and its dissolution in the sixteenth. The results showed a 95% probability that the bone samples dated from around AD1430-1460, and over in Oxford the results both came out at around AD1412-1449, again with a 95% confidence.

Oh dear. However, all was not lost. The proportion of Carbon 14 in the atmosphere, and hence in living things, is not constant but varies over the centuries, and it also varies between the atmosphere and the oceans. Radiocarbon dating of marine organisms can be out by up to several hundred years, and this effect can occur to a lesser degree in terrestrial life where sea-food forms part of the diet. The mass spectrometry of the Grey Friars bone samples reveals that the individual in question had a high-protein diet including a significant proportion of seafood. This would seem reasonable for a medieval nobleman, and certainly for a member of the royal family. Allowing for this, statistical modelling gives the approximate date as AD1475-1530 (with a 69% confidence). This does not prove that the bones are those of Richard III. What it does is remove one possibility which could have proved that these are *not* his remains. And it also tells us something about what he had for supper.

DNA Analysis

Michael Ibsen and Wendy Duldig are descendants in the female line from Richard's eldest sister, Anne, Duchess of Exeter, so their mitochondrial DNA (mt-DNA) should match Richard's – if it was his skeleton and if a sample of DNA could be retrieved from a tooth. Even so, the result might not be conclusive; some versions of mtDNA are very common. But the skeletal results were good: it carried mtDNA haplotype J1C2C – a rare type found in only 1-2% of the population. And it did match the samples taken from Michael and Wendy. To err on the side of caution – bearing in mind the somewhat feminine characteristics of the skeleton, the Y chromosome was also isolated: yes, the body was definitely male.

An official announcement was made on the 4th February 2013 by the University of Leicester at a press conference. Richard Buckley – who had to 'eat his hat' after all, declared:

It is the academic conclusion of the University of Leicester that the individual exhumed at The Greyfriars in August 2012 is indeed King Richard III, the last Plantagenet King of England.

This was followed by a 1½ hour documentary on Channel 4 which included the revelation of a forensic facial reconstruction, done by Caroline Wilkinson of the University of Dundee and funded by the Richard III Society. Hair style and colour, skin complexion and eyes were based on the image of Richard in a Tudor copy of a contemporary portrait, now in the National Portrait Gallery; the computerised version of the excavated skull, adjusted to size, also fitted over the portrait extremely well.

The reconstruction shows Richard as a young man in his early thirties (as he should be) without the crow's-feet and deep worry lines shown in the Tudor portrait. Such surface features would not have affected the skull at all: double chins, wrinkles, blemishes, moles and superficial scars leave no trace in the bone. By 1485, Richard had been king for two traumatic years, was recently bereaved of both his only son and his wife and may well have suffered decades of pain from his scoliosis. Therefore, I wouldn't be surprised if the worried, older-looking face in the Tudor portrait wasn't a truer image of the man than the reconstruction. Even so, it's a fair likeness, though the eyebrows definitely do need a trim.

Recent isotope analysis carried out on Richard's teeth revealed that his food consumption changed significantly in the last two years of his life – after he became king – from a rather plain diet to one that included 'swan, crane, heron and copious amounts of wine'. As for his appearance, according to Dr Turi King, further DNA analysis now indicates a 96% probability that Richard had blue eyes and a 77% chance that his hair was blond as a child but darkened as he grew up (*Ricardian Bulletin,* March 2015), so his facial reconstruction has been redone.

Even more intriguing is the study of his Y chromosome – the one that determines a boy baby and is passed from father to son. Richard's Y chromosome should have matched those of his five living relatives in the male line but it doesn't. Somewhere down the line a wife committed adultery. Joanna Laynesmith (*Ricardian Bulletin,* March 2015) suggests it was Richard's grandfather, Richard of Conisborough, Earl of Cambridge, who was sired by someone other than his mother's husband, Edmund of Langley, Duke of York. This wouldn't have altered our Richard's right to be king since the Yorkist claim came through the female line of his grandmother, Anne Mortimer. It would also solve a number of mysteries if Richard's Y chromosome could be compared a) to that of those 'Princes in the Tower' in Westminster Abbey, b) to that of his brother Edward IV, buried at Windsor, who was rumoured not to be the son of their father, Richard of York, and c) to the remains of Richard Plantagenet of Eastwell in Kent, supposedly King Richard's illegitimate son. So many questions could be answered and, probably, so many new cans of worms might be opened.

The Richard III Society

In 1924 Saxon Barton, a Liverpool surgeon, together with a small group of like-minded friends, formed 'The Fellowship of the White Boar'. They felt history had been unfair to Richard's reputation and wanted to encourage further research. In the 1950s, interest grew with the publication of Josephine Tey's novel *The Daughter of Time*. The mid 1950s also saw the release of Lawrence Olivier's film of Shakespeare's *Richard III* and the publication of Paul Murray Kendall's sympathetic eponymous biography. In 1959 the Fellowship was renamed 'The Richard III Society'. Membership grew, encouraged in the 1980s by Sharon Penman's popular novel *The Sunne in Splendour* and Channel 4's mock *Trial of Richard III* with David Starkey as chief witness for the prosecution.

1985 saw the 500th anniversary of the Battle of Bosworth. The Society now has thousands of members around the world. It holds annual research weekends and triennial conferences; conducts research projects, encourages publications and sponsors university bursaries. Enthusiastic members conduct individual research and share their theories and discoveries, leading to a better understanding of the period.

Conclusion

Whatever else this booklet may achieve, it seems to exonerate Henry Tudor as the possible murderer of the two Little Princes in the Tower. In fact, it seems probable that nobody murdered those two boys but rather they lived on, possibly in Burgundy, until they were each of an age to plague Henry as Pretenders to the throne of England. Richard III certainly did have a spinal deformity, just as Tudor sources say, but definitely not a withered arm. He seemed to be a good king regarding justice and mercy, but made mistakes, which he paid for with both his life and his reputation. As for his true character, that may remain an enigma forever.

The 26th March 2015 saw the reburial of King Richard's remains in Leicester Cathedral and yet another source of controversy: should the service have been a Roman Catholic mass, should he be buried in an Anglican church and why in Leicester and not Westminster or York? Why did he get an ultramodern style tombstone? The arguments will go on, no doubt, so it seems that our 'King of Controversy' hasn't finished with history yet.

Bibliography

A L Rowse: *Bosworth Field & The Wars of the Roses*

Anne Sutton, P.W. Hammond (Ed.): *The Coronation of Richard III*

Annette Carson: *Richard III the Maligned King*

Anthony Cheetham: *Life and Times of Richard III*

Anthony Pollard: *Richard III & The Princes in the Tower*

Audrey Williamson: *The Mystery of the Princes*

Caroline Halsted: *Richard III (volume 1 & 2)*

Charles Ross: *Richard III*

David Baldwin: *Richard III*

David Baldwin: *The Lost Prince*

David Hipshon: *Richard III*

Desmond Seward: *Richard III: England's Black Legend*

Diana Kleyn: *Richard of England*

Dominic Mancini: *The Usurpation of Richard III*

Elizabeth Jenkins: *The Princes in the Tower*

George Buck: *The History of the Life and Reigne of Richard III*

Hammond & Sutton: *Richard III: The Road to Bosworth Field*

Horace Walpole: *The Historic Doubts on the Life and Reign of Richard the Third*

Hugh Ross Williamson: *Historical Enigmas*

James Gairdner: *The History of the Life and Reign of Richard the Third*

Jeremy Potter: *Good King Richard?*

Jeremy Potter: *Pretenders*

John Ashdown Hill: *Eleanor the Secret Queen*

John Ashdown-Hill: *The Last Days of Richard III*

John Ashdown-Hill: *The Mythology of the 'Princes in the Tower'*

Josephine Tey: *The Daughter of Time*

Josephine Wilkinson: *Richard the Young King To Be*

LWT Production for Channel 4: *The Trial of Richard III*

Mary O'Regan: *Richard III: A Brief Life*

Matthew Lewis: *Richard III: Loyalty Binds Me*

Matthew Lewis: *The Survival of the Princes in the Tower*

Michael Hicks: *Edward V*

Paul Murray Kendall: *Richard the Third*

Paul Murray Kendall: *The Great Debate (More and Walpole)*

Peter A Hancock: *Richard III and the Murder in the Tower*

Peter Hammond: *Richard III and the Bosworth Campaign*

Pitkin Guide: *Richard III*

Philippa Langley: *The Princes in the Tower*

P.J. Langley, A.J. Carson (Ed.): *Finding Richard III: The Official Account*

Sharon Penman: *The Sunne in Slendour*

Sir Clements Markham: *Richard III: His Life and Character*

The Rous Roll

Thomas More: *The History of Richard III*

V B Lamb: *The Betrayal of Richard III*

William Shakespeare: *Richard III*

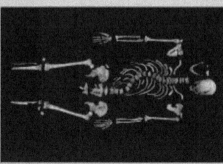

Facial Reconstruction
(University of Dundee)

Skeleton of Richard III
(University of Leicester)

Greyfriers Car Park
(Robinj Leicester pd)